Dwight D. Eisenhower:
Man of Many Hats

with a message from
John S. D. Eisenhower

Written by
Kenneth M. Deitch and JoAnne B. Weisman

Illustrated by
Jay Connolly

Discovery Enterprises, Ltd., Lowell, Massachusetts

© JoAnne B. Weisman, 1990

ISBN 1-878668-02-1 hard cover/library edition
Library of Congress Catalog Card Number 90-82588

10   9   8   7   6   5   4   3   2   1

Printed in the United States of America

A Word on the Literature

For adults seeking further information on Eisenhower, here are a few suggestions. A fine short book is: Robert F. Burk, *Dwight D. Eisenhower: Hero and Politician* (Twayne Publishers, 1986). Stephen E. Ambrose's two-volume biography is excellent. Volume One is, *Eisenhower: Soldier, General of the Army, President-Elect, 1890-1952* (Simon & Schuster, 1983). Volume Two is, *Eisenhower: The President* (Simon and Schuster, 1984).

A nice presentation directed to young adults is: Peter Lars Sandberg, *Dwight D. Eisenhower* (Chelsea House Publishers, 1986). By Dwight D. Eisenhower himself, see those books referred to in the text and also some more informal reminiscences in, *At Ease: Stories I Tell to Friends* (Eastern Acorn Press, 1989). A wonderful account of D-Day is still: Cornelius Ryan, *The Longest Day: June 6, 1944* (Simon and Schuster, 1959). From the books by John S. D. Eisenhower, a good one with which to start is, *Strictly Personal* (Doubleday & Company, 1974). In *Eisenhower: At War, 1943-1945* (Random House, 1986), David Eisenhower has written extensively about his famous grandfather at the height of his military leadership during wartime.

Credits

Title page: Insignia (clockwise from top left), Abilene High School (from 1909); U.S. Military Academy at West Point; Department of the Army; Seal of the President of the United States; SHAPE; and Columbia University. *Photos:* All photos courtesy of Dwight D. Eisenhower Library, Abilene, KS; and Eisenhower National Historic Site, National Military Park, Gettysburg, PA, except as noted. *Cover:* Middle right, Columbia University Library; Bottom, left, Wide World Photos. *Text:* Pages 10, 28 (top), and on p. 47 (right), U.S. Military Academy at West Point; p. 34, Columbia University. *Note:* The painting of the mulberry on page 27 is based on an oil painting by Dwight Shepler, Combat Art Section, U.S. Navy. *Book design:* Jeffrey Pollock. *Typography:* Nancy Myers. *Production:* Phyllis Dougherty

Acknowledgments

Special thanks to the following for their help and support in this project:
Abraham Shamasian
Richard P. Taffe
The Honorable Maxwell M. Rabb
Wolf ColorPrint, Newington, CT

John S. D. Eisenhower

This book tells you about the life of my father, General Dwight D. Eisenhower, Thirty-fourth President of the United States.

During Eisenhower's early years as an officer of the United States Army, he studied and worked hard, waiting for the day, if it should ever come, when he would have to fight to defend the United States against a foreign enemy.

In December of 1941 the United States was swept into a great war, World War II. Within the next year, under Eisenhower's command, the Americans and British began to fight back against the dictators, Adolf Hitler and Benito Mussolini, in North Africa and later in Europe. The war ended in 1945, and Eisenhower was later elected President.

Dwight Eisenhower never expected to be President. He did not even expect to be a general. But he always did his job because he considered it important. He always knew that many others besides himself brought about the victory in World War II. I hope that this book will help you understand him.

John Eisenhower

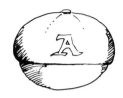

Growing Up in Abilene

Dwight David Eisenhower grew up during the twilight of the nineteenth century and the dawn of the twentieth in a small town in Kansas that was a part of America's rural heartland. Well prepared during his youth to meet the challenges that would follow, he went on to serve the nation for half a century and to become one of the greatest leaders in its history.

He was born in Denison, Texas on October 14, 1890, in the presidency of Benjamin Harrison. He was actually named David Dwight, the David after his father. However, when he was still a baby, his mother, Ida, reversed his given names so that there would not be two Davids around the house.

Before Dwight was a year old, his family moved to Abilene, Kansas. For his father, David, it was a homecoming. He had first arrived in Abilene at the age of fourteen when his own father, Jacob, had brought the family west from Pennsylvania. Then, as a young man, David had ventured off to Texas to search for work. Now, in 1891, he was bringing his family—Ida and their three young boys—back. David went to work in the creamery of the Belle Springs Dairy, and although he never earned more than one hundred dollars per month, the work there proved to be steady.

Ida and David's first home for their family in Abilene was small. In 1898 they moved nearby to a larger house on a little farm that included a barn and three acres of land. By the following year there were six boys in the family—a seventh had died quite young—and the more spacious surroundings of the farmhouse were very welcome.

The farm, run by Ida, provided most of the family's food. In addition to the farm animals, which were a source of milk, meat, and eggs, there was an orchard which provided apples, cherries, grapes, and pears. In the vegetable garden, each boy had a small plot of his own where he could raise vegetables to sell. The farm made the family almost totally self-sufficient. Rarely did the Eisenhowers need to buy anything at the grocery store other than salt, sugar, flour, and kerosene.

Dwight, back row right, with his parents and two brothers

The Eisenhower farm-house in Abilene

Dwight's fifth grade class. He is in the front row, second from left.

David and Ida both worked hard to support their family. She greeted her daily chores with a wide smile and a twinkle in her eye. David, however, was a stern and serious man. He excelled in Greek and enjoyed reading his Greek Bible. In the evening he often read aloud to his sons from the family Bible. But he rarely smiled. Ida raised her boys with a bright and gentle spirit that balanced the strict discipline they received from their father.

For the Eisenhower boys, it was a life rich in many significant ways. Long afterwards, Dwight said: "I have found out in later years we were very poor, but the glory of America is we didn't know it then. All that we knew was that our parents, of great courage, could say to us: Opportunity is all about you. Reach out and take it."

Abilene was a small town of about 3500 people. The railroad tracks divided it into the north side, where the wealthier families lived in large homes with comfortable porches and gracious lawns, and the south side, where the less well-to-do families, like the Eisenhowers, lived more modestly. The town was like an extended family where everyone knew everyone else.

The daily train was Abilene's main link to the world beyond. It brought in supplies and carried away wheat. The town's prosperity depended on two forces outside the control of anyone in Abilene: the weather and the price of wheat.

Dwight was called "Little Ike," and his older brother Edgar was nick-named "Big Ike." Little Ike was an energetic fellow who enjoyed a good fight in the school yard. He loved the outdoors and spent much of his free time hunting, fishing, and exploring. His favorite after-school activities were football and baseball. In sports Ike had both a competitive spirit and a deep sense of the importance of fair play. Sports made him very much aware of the power of teamwork to get things done, a lesson which stayed with him throughout his life.

Ike and his friends on
a camping trip

Heading for West Point

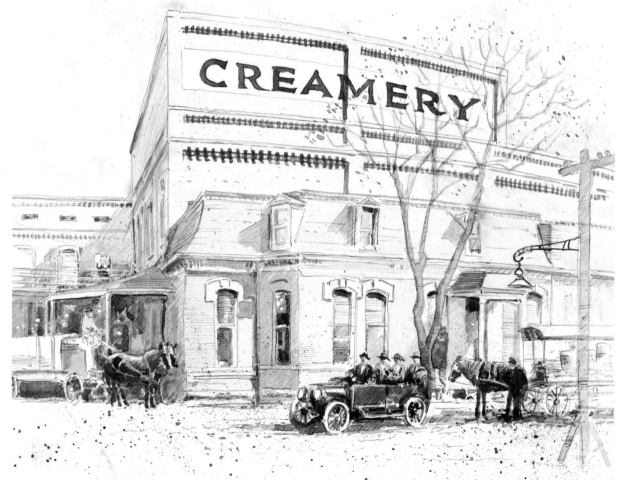

CREAMERY

Abilene H.S. baseball
team

The Belle Springs Dairy,
where Ike and his father
both worked

Dwight was a good student. Military history particularly interested him, and he often studied it on his own. In his senior yearbook it was predicted that he would become a professor of history at Yale.

Edgar and Dwight both graduated from Abilene High School in 1909. When Edgar went off to the University of Michigan, Dwight went to work at the creamery to earn money to help him pay for college. Edgar promised to return the favor. Eventually, Ike became the night manager of the creamery, working from six o'clock in the evening until six in the morning seven days a week and earning ninety dollars a month.

Everett "Swede" Hazlett was a hometown friend of Ike's. He had been away at military school and now was preparing to enter the United States Naval Academy at Annapolis. He visited Ike in the evenings at the creamery, and the two talked about the military for hours. Late at night they would go to the boiler room and fry eggs on a brightly polished shovel. Then, for dessert, the two boys would enjoy ice cream from the dairy.

Swede interested Ike in the idea of attending a military academy. It was the United States Military Academy at West Point to which he gained admission. West Point was free, so Edgar did not have to work in order to help Ike pay his college expenses. Later, Ike would say with amusement that Edgar still owed him one year's hard labor.

In June of 1911, Ike left home and headed east for West Point. He was approaching his adventure with enthusiasm and confidence, and as he boarded the train, he broke into one of his big grins. Some time later, Milton, his youngest brother, told Ike that, back at home later that day, for the first time in his life, he had heard their mother cry.

West Point

I n 1911, attending college was unusual. At that time, fewer than
ten percent of America's youth even graduated from high school.

West Point is a very special college. To fight wars, America has
relied largely upon citizen-soldiers. These are people who enter the military
in time of war and leave it when the war ends, returning to their lives as
civilians. But to be well prepared, America also needs professional officers
for whom the Army is a career. West Point's job is to train them.

West Point is located in a beautiful setting, high above the banks of
the Hudson River, about fifty miles north of New York City.

His first day at the Academy reminded Ike clearly that he was on
the lowest rung of the regular military officers' ladder. Along with the other

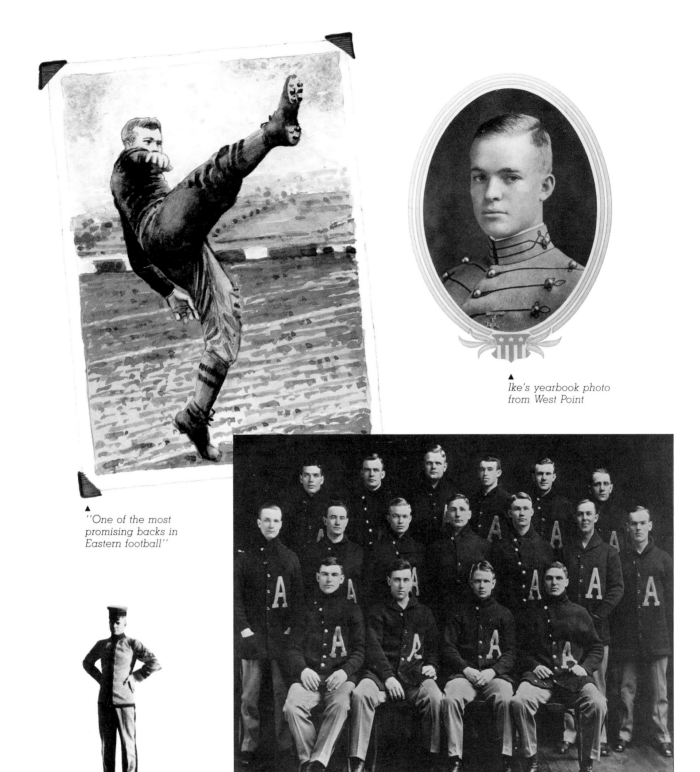

"One of the most
promising backs in
Eastern football"

Ike's yearbook photo
from West Point

As a cadet

Class of 1915 at West Point,
wearers of the "A". Ike is
in the second row, third
from left.

plebes—first-year cadets—he was required to take many orders, which, in some cases, did not seem to make sense. Being ordered to move about "on the double"—quickly—was standard. So was being told to "brace"—stand stiffly, with shoulders very far back, for long periods of time. At nearly twenty-one, Ike was older and more rugged than many of his classmates, and he took these things in stride, sometimes even seeing them as funny.

On the evening of that first day, Ike, along with his classmates, was sworn in to the United States Army. This ceremony, which placed him in the nation's service, moved him deeply, and he always remembered it with great feeling.

Despite his sense of pride in being a part of West Point, Ike did not give in easily to the Academy's strict rules of discipline. He was still full of youthful pranks and mischief. On one occasion he and a fellow student were ordered to report in "full-dress coats." They did just that, arriving in their coats with absolutely nothing else on. They were disciplined, but Ike thought his friends' laughter made it all worthwhile.

Ike made the varsity football team as a yearling—a second-year cadet—but had to stop playing because of a knee injury received in the Tufts game. Before his career ended, however, he had gained some major attention. *The New York Times* had carried a photograph of him punting a football and had called him "one of the most promising backs in Eastern football." Because he wasn't able to play football any more, Ike became a cheerleader, which not only kept him involved with the team, but gave him experience in rallying enthusiasm from the entire corps of cadets in the grandstand.

The class of 1915, Ike's class, is among West Point's most famous. It has been called "the class the stars fell on" because so many graduates —fifty-nine in all—rose to the rank of Brigadier General or higher, which earned them the right to wear one or more stars.

Because West Point was so demanding, not everyone who entered also finished. Ike, who studied civil and military engineering, ranked around the middle of his class. But there was more to it than just grades. One officer wrote that Ike "was born to command." On June 12, 1915, he graduated, and in September was commissioned a Second Lieutenant. An important part of his training had ended. He was now a young officer in the United States Army.

Commander in Preparation

T he most significant moments in Eisenhower's entire career occurred on the 3rd, 4th, 5th, and 6th of June in 1944. Everything before led up to them. Everything after led away. When he graduated from West Point, those moments were almost exactly twenty-nine years in the future. He travelled over a long path to prepare for them.

His first assignment took Ike back to Texas, the state where he had been born. He was stationed for two years at Fort Sam Houston in San Antonio where he continued to learn about life in the Army. And soon after his arrival, he met the young woman who captured his heart and whom he married nine months later.

Her name was Mary Geneva Doud, but she was called Mamie. She had come to San Antonio from Denver for the social season. Ike liked her immediately and wanted to see her as much as possible. Mamie was very popular, but Ike soon persuaded her to make dates only with him. On Valentine's Day of 1916, four months after they had met, he proposed, and she accepted. For their engagement, he gave her his West Point ring.

On July 1st, they were married in her family's home in Denver. Ike wore his tropical dress uniform, so white and so crisp that he decided to remain standing. On their way back to San Antonio, the newlyweds stopped in Abilene so that Mamie could meet Ike's family. Mamie, who had two sisters, was a big hit when she exclaimed, ''At last I have some brothers!'' Ida fixed them all a big fried chicken breakfast.

During those early days of Ike's career and marriage, a major war was being fought in Europe. Now known as World War I, it had begun in August of 1914, almost a year before Ike's graduation from West Point. President Woodrow Wilson hoped to keep America out of the war, but that result was not to be. In April of 1917, America entered the war to support Great Britain, France, and Russia—the Allies.

With his country at war, Ike wanted to sail immediately for France, but was given assignments in the United States instead. Twice he was

John, at 18 months,
with Mamie

Ike and Mamie

Icky

Insignia of Commissioned Officers
United States Army

General
of the Army (GA)

General (GEN)

Lieutenant General
(LTG)

Major General
(MG)

Brigadier General
(BG)

Colonel (COL)

Lieutenant Colonel
(LTC)

Major (MAJ)

Captain (CPT)

First Lieutenant
(1LT)

Second Lieutenant
(2LT)

scheduled to sail, but both times the plans were cancelled, the second time because, on November 11, 1918, the war had ended. He had missed it. For Eisenhower, who had chosen a military career, this outcome was deeply disappointing.

The Army adjusted to peacetime by shrinking rapidly. During the war its members had numbered well over two million. By mid-1920, only about 204,000 soldiers were on active duty, and the Army's size remained small over the next twenty years. Ike continued to gain experience. One lesson he learned was that promotions come more slowly in peace than in war. His rise to Major in 1920 was to be his last promotion for sixteen years.

One of Ike's early postwar experiences came during the summer of 1919 in the first transcontinental motorized convoy. Seventy-two vehicles and 280 men drove from Washington, D.C. to San Francisco, California. Because cars and trucks and even the nation's roads were all still in their early stages, the convoy travelled at only ten to fifteen miles per hour. The trip took nearly two months. Writing about it afterwards, Ike concluded: "...efforts should be made to get our people interested in producing better roads."

In the early years of Ike and Mamie's marriage, their children were born. John Sheldon Doud Eisenhower was born on August 3, 1922. He was to follow in many of his father's footsteps by attending West Point and then spending much of his career in the nation's service. He became a Brigadier General in the Army and later was America's Ambassador to Belgium. John was Ike and Mamie's second son. Doud Dwight Eisenhower, born on September 24, 1917, and nicknamed "Icky," had been their first child. He died when he was only three. Icky's death was devastating, and for the half century to follow, Ike always sent Mamie flowers on Icky's birthday.

A year after Icky's death, Ike went to Panama where he would serve for three years under the command of General Fox Conner, a scholarly soldier and a southern gentleman who encouraged him to study military history. Later in life Ike said: "Fox Conner was the ablest man I ever knew."

General Conner helped Ike get into the Army's Command and General Staff School at Fort Leavenworth in Kansas. At West Point, he had been in the second quarter of his class, but at the Command and General Staff School, he ranked first in a class made up of 245 of the most promising officers in the Army.

In 1928, Ike began a second assignment abroad: fifteen months in Paris. The Eisenhowers liked to entertain and, as in other places where they had lived, their apartment on Pont Mirabeau came to be called "Club Eisenhower." In 1944, sixteen years after he first reached France, Ike would set foot on French soil once again, but under enormously different circumstances.

From Paris, the Eisenhowers returned to Washington where Ike was stationed for the next six years. The nation was suffering through the Great Depression, and many, many people were unemployed. As an Army officer, Ike did not have to face that difficult situation himself.

In the fall of 1930, General Douglas MacArthur became the Army's Chief of Staff, and a while later, Ike began to work closely under him, helping to make plans for the nation in case of war. Ike became MacArthur's personal assistant. His job included helping MacArthur try to get more money for the Army so that it could have better, more modern equipment.

When his time as Chief of Staff came to an end in 1935, MacArthur was invited to help build an army for the Philippines, which was getting ready for its independence from the United States. He asked Ike to join him. Ike's assignment there lasted four years. During that time, he was promoted to Lieutenant Colonel, his first promotion since 1920. While in the Philippines, he also learned to fly an airplane which, as well as helping him travel around to make inspections, was also fun.

Mamie and John joined Ike in the Philippines many months after his arrival. For Mamie the stay was unpleasant, but for John it was an excellent experience. His years there were "among the happiest" in his life.

One of his goals in the Army, Ike told John, was "to make everybody I worked for regretful when I was ordered to other duty." In the Philippines he achieved that goal. When the Eisenhowers left by ship in December of 1939, not only was MacArthur very sorry to see Ike go, but so was Manuel Quezon, the Philippines' leader with whom he had worked closely.

Ike was more than ready to leave. When his new orders came through, he welcomed them. Later, after learning of Germany's attack on Poland on September 1, 1939—the beginning of World War II—Ike became even more intent on leaving. He had missed the previous war, and now, within a year, he would be fifty years old. If America was going to fight in this war, Ike wanted to be present to take his part.

Ike and MacArthur in
the Philippines, 1935

Ike visited the flight
school in Panama. Some
years later, he took fly-
ing lessons and received
his pilot's license in the
Philippines. He was the
first American President
who could pilot a plane.

President Quezon smiles
as Mamie pins a medal
on Ike.

Hitler and the Third Reich

A dolf Hitler gained control of Germany in 1933 when his political party, the Nazi Party, came to power. Germany under Hitler is often called the Third Reich.

Hitler's thinking was twisted. He believed that Aryans made up a race of superior people, better than all others, especially Jews. To Hitler the term "Aryan" more or less meant someone German or, at least in his mind, German-like.

During the Third Reich, many of Hitler's warped ideas came to be expressed in brutal actions. To pursue their monstrous ambitions, the Nazis killed around eleven million innocent people. Jews were the people they hated most, but they killed millions of non-Jews, too.

Expanding Germany's territory was another aim of the Nazis. They wanted to gain more *lebensraum*—"living space." The Third Reich's attack on Poland, which started World War II, was only the latest among Nazi Germany's aggressive acts against neighboring land. In 1936 Hitler had moved troops west across the Rhine River into an area where they were not supposed to be. In 1938 he had forced Austria to become part of the Third Reich. Later that year he had taken over one part of Czechoslovakia, and in 1939 he added the rest of it.

Great Britain and France could no longer stand by and watch Hitler's Germany cruelly take advantage of weaker nations. Two days after the invasion of Poland, they each declared war on Germany. The battle lines were drawn.

A swastika, the Nazi symbol, is represented in the flag below. ▼

Countries Controlled by the Axis at its Maximum in World War II

Countries under occupation and/or controlled by the Axis, 1939-1945

Farthest extent of Hitler's invasion of the Soviet Union

Sweden

Finland

Norway

Estonia

Denmark

Latvia

Lithuania

Great Britain

East Prussia

Union of Soviet Socialist Republics (Russia)

Holland

Belgium   Germany

Poland

Czechoslovakia

France

Austria

Switzerland

Hungary

Rumania

Portugal

Yugoslavia

Spain

Italy

Bulgaria

Albania

Turkey

Greece

Morocco

Algeria

Tunisia

Libya

Egypt

◄ *Adolf Hitler*

Rise to Wartime Leadership

Eisenhower had returned to the United States from the Philippines three months after the start of the war in Europe. America was not yet directly at war, but it needed to get ready. Eisenhower's job was to help the country prepare. Soon after his return, he was sent to Fort Lewis in the state of Washington. There he got the kind of assignment he really wanted—commanding troops. Strong and healthy, he was happy to be working closely with troops, "soldiering," rather than being tied to a "desk job."

In the summer of 1941 an opportunity to show his skills as a military leader came his way. General George C. Marshall, the Army's Chief of Staff, had ordered a large war game. Called the "Louisiana maneuvers," it was serious practice for real war. Around 400,000 troops participated. The U.S. Second Army was to defend Louisiana against the Third Army's attack. With Eisenhower as its main planner, the Third Army won a clear victory. Almost immediately afterwards, Eisenhower was promoted to Brigadier General.

Three months later, America was really at war. On December 7, 1941, Japanese planes suddenly turned a peaceful Sunday morning in Hawaii into a disaster by launching a surprise attack against the American naval base at Pearl Harbor. President Roosevelt called the day "a date that will live in infamy." Japan was on the same side as Germany and Italy, and the three together were called the "Axis." Within a matter of days, America was at war with all of them.

General Marshall quickly summoned Eisenhower to Washington, thinking that his experience in the Philippines would make him a valued adviser. Soon most of Eisenhower's attention was focused on the war in Europe which had already been going on for over two years. During that time, the Third Reich had expanded very far in many directions. It had conquered vast areas of Europe and had also moved into North Africa to come to the aid of the Italians. The Germans had not succeeded in invading Great Britain, but for a long time they had bombed it heavily. Hitler's enemies needed help, and early in 1942, Eisenhower concluded: "We've got to go to Europe and fight...."

▲ Above: During the Louisiana maneuvers, Ike (right) briefed Maj. Gen. H. A. Dargue (left) and Lt. Gen. Leslie McNair.

▲ Pearl Harbor in Hawaii was attacked on December 7, 1941.

From Gibraltar, Ike was able to see American and British ships crossing the Mediterranean to North Africa.

General George C. Marshall, Army Chief of Staff, met with Ike in Algiers in June, 1943.

Early in June, Eisenhower returned from a quick trip to Europe. Three weeks later, he was heading there again, this time to stay. General Marshall had appointed him commander of the European Theater of Operations, placing Ike in charge of all American military personnel within it.

The time had arrived to reverse the direction of the war and to begin the long struggle to free Europe from the Nazis. Because of the strong defenses which Hitler's forces had built, the continent of Europe was sometimes called Fortress Europe. This name suggested how difficult it would be to mount a successful invasion.

Gaining control of North Africa was the first step. This Allied British and American effort was given the code name Torch, and Eisenhower was chosen to command it. He went to Gibraltar, a spot well located for directing the invasion. Because it was in a war zone, his headquarters was located underground. Damp caves served as offices.

On November 8, 1942, the invasion began. The fighting lasted six months, longer than was originally hoped, but the Allies were successful in driving the Axis out of North Africa.

The next step was to free Europe itself. The Allies first entered the Continent on the Italian peninsula. To get there, they had used the islands of Pantelleria and Sicily as stepping-stones. Once again, Ike commanded the British and American forces. There was concern that taking Pantelleria, which was valuable for its airfield, would be costly, but the island fell easily on June 11, 1943. Taking Sicily was different. Following its invasion on July 7th, six weeks passed before it was brought securely under Allied control.

The Italian mainland was the next objective. Shortly after the Allies had heavily bombed Rome in mid-July, Benito Mussolini, the Italian dictator fighting on Hitler's side, was overthrown. The new Italian government soon surrendered to the Allies, but because troops of the Third Reich were occupying the country, Italy still had to be invaded. The first Allied landings came near Italy's southern tip on September 3rd, and others followed elsewhere in southern Italy. For months the Allies battled their way northward against strong resistance. Although Rome did not actually fall until early in June of 1944, the outlook for victory in Italy had become clear much earlier. When it did, many senior Allied commanders shifted their attention to the next major objective: the invasion of the Continent across the English Channel.

Overlord

Overlord was the code name for the entire plan to invade France from Great Britain and to free the rest of Europe from the Nazis. President Roosevelt was to choose Overlord's commander. He and Eisenhower met in North Africa on December 7, 1943, and he gave Ike the news: "Well, Ike, you'd better start packing, you are going to command Overlord."

With Overlord's pressures lying ahead for Eisenhower, General Marshall insisted that Ike get at least a brief change of scene while he could. Early in January, he travelled to the United States, his first visit home in a little over a year and a half. He had a round of meetings, a reunion with family in Kansas, and an all-too-brief few days with Mamie.

Around mid-month he returned to Britain where his headquarters, known as SHAEF, Supreme Headquarters Allied Expeditionary Force, was located. Over 16,000 personnel would come to work at SHAEF for the planning of Overlord.

The orders Eisenhower had received were simple and direct: "You will enter the continent of Europe and, in conjunction with the other Allied nations, undertake operations aimed at the heart of Germany and the destruction of her armed forces." The planning required to carry out these orders was a huge task.

D-Day, the name reserved for the day of the invasion, had to be chosen carefully. It had to be late enough in the year to allow preparations to be completed, but early enough to give the Allied forces several months in Europe before the arrival of winter weather. The moon and tides also had to be right. Together these conditions narrowed down the possible times for an invasion in 1944 to three: at the beginning of May or during the first or the third week in June. Although the weather was not predictable long in advance, the invasion could not be launched unless it was favorable when the chosen time arrived.

President Roosevelt told Eisenhower he would be commanding Overlord.

The subway stations in London served as bomb shelters during the war.

The date originally selected was May 1st, but before the end of January it was changed to June 5th because of the scarcity of landing craft. This delay allowed an extra month for producing even more new landing craft, and Eisenhower thought the change was of great importance.

A site for the invasion also had to be chosen. Calais in France was the most obvious possibility. Only twenty-one miles across the English Channel from Dover, it is the place in Europe closest to Britain. The Germans expected General George Patton, an American and one of the best known Allied generals, to command the invasion's leading troops. By placing him quite visibly in Dover at the head of an army, the Allies were trying to make the Germans believe that the landing would take place around Calais. In fact, General Patton was a decoy, and much of the equipment with which he appeared to be supplied, including tanks and landing craft, was fake.

The site actually selected was a section of the coast southwest from Calais and over one hundred miles away at its nearest point. Located on the coast of Normandy, a region of France, it is about sixty miles wide. The invasion would take place there on five beaches called, from west to east: Utah, Omaha, Gold, Juno, and Sword.

For months the preparations went forward in high gear. By the beginning of June a huge force had been assembled. Eisenhower was in command of almost three million Allied troops. There were Americans, British, and Canadians. France, Czechoslovakia, Belgium, Norway, and Holland were also represented. The force for the invasion itself consisted of approximately 4,000 ships, 176,000 men, 20,000 vehicles, and 12,000 aircraft. Southern England was sealed off; only those involved in launching the invasion could come and go.

On the evening of June 3rd, Eisenhower gave the order, and ships began to cross the English Channel. But the weather was bad and showed no sign of improving. Around 4 A.M. on the 4th, Ike made the agonizing decision to postpone D-Day for twenty-four hours. The ships returned.

On the evening of the 4th, they set out again. Around 4 A.M. on the 5th, Ike faced the critical decision once more. But this time there were two differences. Though far from ideal, the weather was more promising than it had been twenty-four hours earlier, and a postponement, if ordered now, would have to be for almost two weeks, not just one day.

ENGLAND

London

Southampton

Portsmouth

Dover •

• Calais

Portland •

ENGLISH CHANNEL

Utah Omaha Gold Juno Sword

Le Havre •

Seine River

NORMANDY

FRANCE

The invading Allied
forces came from
England across the
Channel to the beaches
of Normandy in France.

Complete portable harbors, called mulberries,
were assembled in England and then towed
across the Channel. They were constructed from
huge concrete sections and from the rubble of
buildings bombed in England.

Ike talks to the 101st
Airborne Division of
paratroopers before
the invasion.

General Eisenhower
discusses plans with
British Prime Minister
Winston Churchill.

The Allied soldiers
disembarked from the
landing craft.

Ike was with a small group of his closest senior staff. He invited their thoughts. Finally it was up to him alone. He took the time to make up his mind. Then he gave his decision: ''Okay, we'll go.''

D-Day would be on June 6, 1944.

For Eisenhower, the rest of June 5th was a day largely of waiting. When a bit of sunshine broke through, it cheered his spirit. Before dinner he scribbled a message: ''Our landings...have failed...and I have withdrawn the troops.... The troops...did all that bravery...could do. If any blame or fault attaches to the attempt it is mine alone.'' He put it into his wallet and hoped he would never have to use it.

Early in the evening he travelled with some members of his staff to visit with paratroopers of the 101st Airborne as they were preparing to board their planes. They would parachute in and land behind the beaches before those on the ships came ashore. Only after the last C-47 was in the air did Eisenhower return to his car for the trip back to headquarters. Tears were in his eyes.

In his Order of the Day for D-Day, Eisenhower had told the troops: ''You are about to embark upon the Great Crusade.... The eyes of the world are upon you....''

Around 7 A.M. on D-Day, news began to arrive. Mostly, it was favorable. Casualties were lower than had been expected. By the end of the day, which is sometimes called ''the longest day,'' over 150,000 Allied troops had overcome Hitler's defenses. The invasion had succeeded. Fighting, sacrifice, and tragic loss of life still lay ahead. But now the end was somehow in view.

On June 7th, Eisenhower inspected the site of the landings firsthand. Several days later he brought some of the highest-ranking Allied military leaders, including General Marshall, across the Channel to Omaha Beach. The visit was a sure signal that the Allies' position on the Continent was secure.

A week after D-Day, the beachhead was eight to twelve miles deep and fifty miles wide, and the progress would continue. By late July, over one and one-quarter million Allied troops had landed. On July 25th, Paris was liberated; its occupation by the Nazis had lasted just over four years.

On October 21st, Aachen became the first German city to fall to the Allies. But even though the war was going very much against them, the Germans still had the strength left for one more major offensive. It began on December 16th, took place in Belgium, and was known as the Battle of the Bulge. The "bulge" referred to the indentation the German offensive caused in the Allied lines. The attack caught the Allies by surprise, but Eisenhower showed great skill as a battlefield commander when he organized a powerful counterattack which set the stage for the Allies' final victorious sweep into Germany from the west.

On March 7, 1945, the Allies captured a bridge over the Rhine River at Remagen before the Germans could destroy it. The end for the Third Reich was near. Not only was it under attack from the west, but the Russians were pressing in from the east as well. Americans and Russians finally linked up at the Elbe River on April 25th. Nine days earlier, the Russians had begun their attack to capture Berlin, the German capital, where Hitler was holed up in his bunker. There, on April 30th, with his evil ambitions foiled and his country in ruins and on the verge of total disaster, Hitler shot himself and died.

The Third Reich survived one more week. Its surrender took place in a school in Reims, France, early on the morning of May 7th. When the papers had been signed and all the other details completed, it was then necessary to write an announcement of the long-awaited news. After a number of others had each taken a try, General Eisenhower decided to do it himself: "The mission of this Allied force was fulfilled at 0241 local time, May 7, 1945."

For others, however, there was considerably more to say. Already in December of 1944, Eisenhower had been promoted to the rank of General of the Army, a five-star general. Now, on behalf of all whom General Eisenhower had served, General Marshall wrote to him: "You have completed your mission with the greatest victory in the history of warfare. . . . Through all of this. . .you have been selfless in your actions, always sound and tolerant in your judgments and altogether admirable in the courage and wisdom of your military decisions.

"You have made history, great history for the good of mankind and you have stood for all we hope for and admire in an officer of the United States Army. These are my tributes and my personal thanks."

TODAY IS B-DAY
—7

The Evening Bulletin

V-E EXTRA

Copyright, 1945, by Bulletin Company   Reg. U. S. Pat. Off.

99th YEAR, No. 22   (APRIL CIRCULATION 702,210 COPIES DAILY)   PHILADELPHIA, MONDAY, MAY 7, 1945   Entered as second-class matter Nov. 11, 1887, at the post-office at Philadelphia, Pa., under the Act of Mar. 3, 1879   THREE CENTS

War in Europe Over with Full Surrender

LEGISLATURE ASKS HIGHWAYS INQUIRY; MAY CLOSE TODAY

Probe Action is Condition Under which the House Accepts Gas Tax Shift

SCHOOL BILL IS PASSED

By ROBERT W. COMBER
(Of The Bulletin Staff)

Harrisburg, May 7.—A legislative investigation of the State Highway Department during the remaining 20 months of Governor Martin's Administration was projected as the General Assembly prepared to end its 1945 session today.

Concurrence by the Senate in an eleventh hour resolution adopted by the House of Representatives to authorize the highways inquiry constituted a compromise feature of the House yielding to the upper chamber in the dispute over proceeds of the continued one-cent-a-gallon emergency tax on gasoline collected during the next two fiscal years.

Toward the close end of the Saturday sitting of the House, which did not end until 7 A. M. yesterday, that body voted almost unanimously to accept Senate amendments to the Wood (R-Montgomery) bill limiting to $17,000,000 the amount of that gasoline revenue to be distributed among municipal subdivisions for local street, road and bridge improvements, not retaining remainder of the $22,000,000 total estimated yield in the motor license fund for use by the State Highways Department.

Scope of Inquiry

The resolution sponsored by four House members from rural districts sets up a special committee of five Senators and five Representatives appointed by the presiding officers of each branch, to study highway laws pertaining to duties and powers of the department, and examine regulations, practices and activities of State highway officials in construction and maintenance of roads and bridges.

During the interim until the 1947 Legislature convenes the investigators are authorized to report to the Governor findings and recommendations from time to time, and a final report to the next General Assembly, when the Martin Administration will be going out of office, shall include recommendations on changes deemed desirable to correct any abuses and evils in administration of the department.

Under another part of the agreement, at the instances of House Republicans, the Joint Conference Committee struck from the gasoline tax bill a Senate amendment appropriating $50,000 to the Joint State Government Commission for an investigation to determine the amount of State aid which should be granted to municipalities for highway purposes, and to fix relationship between the Commonwealth and the subdivisions.

(Continued on Page Three, Column Two)

BRITISH CAPTURE JAP GUNS IN BURMA

Calcutta, May 7.—(AP)—British 14th Army troops mopping up the scores of thousands of Japanese soldiers left to fend for themselves in Burma have captured enemy guns and equipment at Tenanama, 27 miles south of Minbu, a Southeast Asia Command communique said today.

LONDON TRANSPORT STRIKE IS ENDED

London, May 7.—(AP)—A five-day old transport strike that tied up bus routes in north and south London ended today as a dispute over working hours was submitted to arbitration.

Victorious Three

Prime Minister
WINSTON CHURCHILL

President
HARRY S. TRUMAN

Associated Press Wirephotos
Premier Marshal
JOSEF STALIN

SGT. J. A. M'GARRITY KILLED ON LUZON

Son of Ex-Assemblyman among 15 on List; 22 are Wounded

Sergeant James A. McGarrity, Jr., 23, one of two sons of former State Representative James A. McCarrity in the service, was killed January 14 on Luzon.

An infantryman, he lived at 5550 Pemberton st. He was graduated from West Catholic High School, and enlisted in July, 1942, after attending La Salle College for one year. He went overseas in April, 1944.

A brother, John J., 27, is a member of the Army Engineers, and has been stationed in Iran for three years. His father, active in Republican politics for more than 20 years, is a train dispatcher for the Pennsylvania Railroad. He was elected to the Legislature in 1938 from the 22d district.

McGarrity was among 15 servicemen from this area listed today as KILLED. Twenty-two others were named as wounded, and eight are known to be missing.

KILLED

Captain Charles F. Sampsel, husband of Mrs. Marion H. Sampsel, 415 Radcliffe st., Bristol, was killed in the Pacific.

Second Lieutenant George A. McClellan, son of Mrs. Augusta A. McClellan, of 441 N. 9th st., Camden, was killed in Europe.

Staff Sergeant Anthony J. Daniels, 30, son of Mrs. Anna N. Yonush, 1415 S. Paxon st., was killed in Italy January 30. A tail gunner, he had completed 54 missions and had been killed for a second tour of duty. He was graduated from West Catholic High School, and attended ...

PENNY CIGARETTES BANNED

OPA Bars Sale of Loose Smokes from Broken Packages

Washington, May 7.—(AP)—OPA today banned the retail sale of loose cigarettes, putting distribution on a full package or nothing basis.

Since the beginning of the current shortage some retailers have curtailed package sales, offering instead individual cigarettes, usually at 1 cent each.

This, OPA said, has resulted in unnecessarily high prices.

THE BULLETIN TODAY

Amusements	14
Crossword Puzzle	14
Death Notices	4, 17
Editorials	8
Evening Chat	6
Financial	16
Health	
Letters and Answers	8 and 20
Opinion and Review	9
Radio	21
Ration Information	10
Serial Story:	
"Leave Her to Heaven"	10
Sports	15, 16
Want Ads	16 to 19
Women's Page	10

World War II Dates—Rise and Fall of Germany

1933—Hitler becomes chancellor.

1934—June 14: Hitler meets Mussolini in Venice to plot seizure of power. August 2: President von Hindenburg dies. Hitler picks up title of reichsfuehrer.

1936—March 7: Hitler sends troops into Rhineland demilitarized by Versailles Treaty; November 25: Germany and Japan sign anti-Comintern pact.

1938—March 12: Hitler swallows up Austria; September 30: Munich accord, okayed by Britain, France and Italy, means kayo for Czechoslavakia, which, October 1, loses Sudetenland.

1939—March 25: Hitler demands of Poland Danzig and corridor across corridor as link to East Prussia; March 31: Britain counters with promise of aid to Poland if Hitler strikes; August 14: Hitler-Stalin friendship pact signed and, September 1: shooting begins in terrific lunge into Poland; September 3: Britain, France declare war; November 30: Russia attacks Finland.

1940—Hitler's successes in one-two-three order amaze world; April 9: Denmark, Norway invaded; May 10: Belgium, Netherlands, Luxembourg invaded; June 22: France, with a "stab in the back" by Italy, collapses; September 1: London air blitz begins.

1941—June 22: Red pact turned into scrap of paper by Hitler's invasion of Russia; October 8: Nazis capture Orel and, November 22: Rostov, 1,000 miles from starting point. November 29: Russians recapture Rostov; December 11: Hitler declares war on U.S., four days after Pearl Harbor.

1942—January 14: sinking of tanker Norness off Long Island starts Atlantic U-boat raids; June 13: Rommel strikes into Egypt; Nov. 1: Eisenhower invades North Africa; November 19: Reds open winter counter-offensive destined to trap 22 Nazi divisions at Stalingrad.

1943—May 12: Axis surrenders in Africa; July 11: Reds open drive that will oust Hitler Orel, Bryansk, Kharkov, Novorossisk, threaten Dnieper River line; July 31: II Duce ousted; September 3: Hitler's fortress wall breached with invasion of Italy, and September 8: Badoglio government surrenders; November—Berlin bombed; November-December—Roosevelt, Churchill and Chiang Kai-shek meet in Cairo followed by "Big Three" session with Stalin at Tehran.

1944—Jan. 27: Leningrad freed by Russians; Feb. 22: Germany bombed for first time by U. S. air forces; May: Allies pound Germany and take toll of France from air all month; June 6: Allies under Eisenhower invade France in greatest land, sea and air invasion in history;

July 12: Patton outflanks St. Lo; August 15: Allies land in southern France; August 25: Paris liberated; December 16: Nazis launch surprise counter-offensive against First American Army; Dec. 19: Panzer units smash through Luxembourg into Belgium; Dec. 24: Patton's 3d Army strikes enemy's flank from south; Dec. 27: Bastogne relieved, Americans encircled there by Nazis, refused to surrender and played vital part in stopping von Rundstedt's drive.

1945—Jan. 10: Germans fall back in Belgium Bulge. Jan. 12: Russians began heavy offensive on East Front; Jan. 23: Russians reach Oder River; Jan. 31: Russians 45 miles from Berlin; March 8: American First Army crosses Rhine at Remagen; March 27: Seven Allied armies fighting east of Rhine; April 12: Roosevelt dies at Warm Springs, Ga.; April 21: 9th Army across Elbe; Patton enters Czechoslovakia; April 25: Russians battling in streets of Berlin, form junction with American army at Torgau; Allied invasion reveals atrocities in Nazi prison camps; April 29: Mussolini slain by Italian Partisans near Milan; May 1: Death of Hitler proclaimed by Admiral Doenitz; May 2: Berlin taken by Russians; German army of Northern Italy surrenders; May 4: Northern Italy surrenders; May 4: Nazis' surrender in Denmark, Holland and northwest Germany.

3D NEARING PRAGUE WHEN END CAME

Gen. Patton had Thrown 250,000 Troops into Final Campaign

By The Associated Press

Paris, May 7.—American and Russian armies were beating through Czechoslovakia and Austria today in the final mopup when the Germans announced their capitulation.

Patriots in Prague aided U. S. Third Army ranks were only 15 miles from that city, largest still in German hands.

General Patton had thrown nearly a quarter of a million Third Army troops into the closing campaign. In advances of up to 25 miles, his tanks and infantry advanced within 50 miles southwest and 52 miles south of the Czech capital.

The German-controlled Prague radio said Marshal Ivan S. Konev's First Ukrainian Army Group had driven into Bohemia from Saxony to a point about 60 or 65 miles north of Prague.

Patriots Engage Germans

Two Russian army groups were pressing in from the east, fighting into the outskirts of the big rail junction of Olmuetz and the Hohen-...

GOERING SEIZED, KIN SAYS

Hitler Had Him Removed From Berchtesgaden, Nephew Asserts

New York, May 7—(AP)—Fritz Goering, nephew of Hermann Goering, said his uncle wanted to make peace ten days ago, and was arrested on Hitler's orders and removed from Berchtesgaden. Mutual correspondent Seymor Korman reported in a broadcast yesterday from Berchtesgaden.

Field Marshal Albert Kesselring fled from Berchtesgaden several days before American troops arrived, young Goering said. He added he did not know where his uncle had been taken.

LEOPOLD REJOINS FAMILY

King Reported in Switzerland and Will Return to Belgium

New York, May 7.—(AP)—The Belgian domestic radio in a broadcast monitored by the FCC, said yesterday that "King Leopold and his family are reunited" and "at the moment are in Switzerland preparing for their return to Belgium."

STILL ON TOP

"War has improved our morals," said B. Heflin Fox, screen writer, "but we Americans are still the world's greatest divorcers.

"Yes," a Frenchman said of us, "I have been married five times, four times in America and once in earnest."

Signing Takes Place at Headquarters of Eisenhower

By The Associated Press

London, May 7—The greatest war in history ended today with the unconditional surrender of Germany.

The surrender of the Reich to the Western Allies and Russia was made at General Eisenhower's headquarters at Reims, France, by Colonel General Gustav Jodl, chief of staff of the German Army.

This was announced officially after German broadcasts told the German people that Grand Admiral Karl Doenitz had ordered the capitulation of all fighting forces, and called off the U-boat war.

Awaited was a formal V-E proclamation from Washington, London and Moscow.

The surrender came at 2.41 A. M., French time (8.41 P. M. Sunday, Eastern War Time) at a little red school house which is the headquarters of General Eisenhower.

It was signed for the Supreme Allied Command by Lieutenant General Walter Bedell Smith, Chief of Staff for General Eisenhower. It was also signed by General Ivan Susloparoff for Russia and by General Francois Sevez for France.

General Eisenhower was not present at the signing, but immediately afterward Jodl and his fellow delegate, General Admiral Hans Georg Friedeburg, were received by the Supreme Commander.

They were asked sternly if they understood the surrender terms imposed upon Germany and if they would be carried out by Germany.

They answered yes.

Joy at the news was tempered only by the realization that the war against Japan remains to re resolved, with many casualties still ahead.

Total Casualties Estimated at 40,000,000

The end of the European warfare, greatest, bloodiest and costliest war in human history—it has claimed at least 40,000,000 casualties on both sides in killed, wounded, and captured—came after five years, eight months, and six days of strife that overspread the globe.

Hitler's arrogant armies invaded Poland on September 1, 1939, beginning the agony that convulsed the world for 2,319 days.

Unconditional surrender of the beaten remnants of his legions first was announced by the Germans.

The historic news began breaking with a Danish broadcast that Norway had been surrendered uncon-...

(Continued on Page Two, Column Two)

REDOUBT ONLY A DREAM

Innsbruck, May 3—(Delayed)—(AP)—Gauleiter Franz Hofen, commander of a section of the surrendered area of Austria, confessed today that the "German national redoubt" amounted to only a dream.

LOCAL WEATHER FORECAST

Issued by the U. S. Weather Bureau at 8 A. M. today: Fair and a little warmer today. Partly cloudy and cool tonight. Tuesday cloudy with occasional showers. Cooler Tuesday afternoon.

WEATHER RECORD MAY 7, 1945

LOST AND FOUND

All across America and the world, newspapers, like The Evening Bulletin, announced the end of the war in Europe. The three Allied leaders shown above are British Prime Minister Winston Churchill; American President Harry S. Truman; and Russian Premier Marshal Josef Stalin.

Eisenhower worked closely with Churchill during the war. President Franklin D. Roosevelt had died on April 12, 1945, shortly before the end of the war in Europe, and Truman became America's new President.

High Honors for the Hero

Even though the fighting went on in the Pacific for three more months after V-E Day—V-E meant Victory in Europe—the end of the war in Europe was still cause for great joy. Eisenhower was at the center of much celebration, ceremony, and thanksgiving over it.

On May 15th, in London, he ate his first meal in a restaurant and attended his first show in three years. When people at the theater recognized him and cheered, he responded to their enthusiastic greeting: "It's nice to be back in a country where I can *almost* speak the language."

London's formal celebration took place in Guildhall on June 12th. Eisenhower arrived in a horse-drawn carriage. During the ceremony he received the Duke of Wellington's sword and made the main speech.

Later in June he returned to the United States. He addressed a joint session of Congress, and its members gave him a standing ovation. That same day he flew to New York where he was honored in a ticker-tape parade. The crowd assembled at City Hall to greet him was estimated at two million.

By November, Eisenhower had become the Army's Chief of Staff, succeeding General Marshall. He served in this position for twenty-seven months, and it brought him to work, once more, in Washington, D.C.

The beginning of the Cold War was capturing Eisenhower's attention. The Cold War is the name for the conflict that developed almost immediately after the end of World War II between America and its allies, on the one hand, and the Soviet Union (Russia) and its allies, on the other. It means unfriendly relations without actual warfare.

During the war a spirit of cooperation had grown between America and the Soviet Union because they were trying together to defeat the Third Reich. Although hopeful that this good spirit would continue, Eisenhower was becoming aware that it was crumbling fast. On March 5, 1946, during a famous speech at Westminster College in Fulton, Missouri, Winston Churchill told the world that "...an *iron curtain* has descended across the Continent."

▲
About two million
people cheered Ike at
a ticker-tape parade in
New York City.

President Truman chats with Ike after appointing him U.S. Army Chief of Staff.

Eisenhower was at Columbia University from June, 1948 through 1950.

Ike shares a happy moment with the Columbia University football team.

In what would become the Cold War's most famous image, Churchill had vividly summarized what Ike and many others were also concluding.

When he stepped down as Chief of Staff early in February of 1948, Eisenhower swore in, as his successor, General Omar Bradley, his close wartime colleague and his classmate at West Point. Just before the transfer of authority, Eisenhower addressed a message "To the American Soldier." It ended this way: "I cannot let this day pass without telling the fighting men —those who have left the ranks and you who still wear the uniform—that my fondest boast shall always be: 'I was their fellow soldier.'"

During the next few months, Eisenhower did most of the work on *Crusade in Europe*, his book about the war. It was highly praised as an important contribution to history. In addition, it brought him some money which was quite welcome because, over the years, he and Mamie had been able to save virtually nothing on Ike's modest military salary.

In June of 1948 they moved to a section of New York City known as Morningside Heights. Columbia University is located there, and Eisenhower was to be its new president.

Columbia is one of the nation's most distinguished universities. Originally called King's College, it is older than the United States itself. When Eisenhower went there, Columbia was within a few years of celebrating its two hundredth anniversary.

Eisenhower had great respect for Columbia. In his short time there, he got a number of programs started that would remain valuable in the life of the University long after he had left. The American Assembly is one. It sponsors meetings at which leaders with diverse backgrounds discuss topics of great public interest, and it arranges to have the results of these gatherings published so that they can be widely shared.

Eisenhower remained at Columbia through the end of 1950. He left for a new and major assignment that President Harry S. Truman wanted him to take on and that required him to be in Europe.

In 1949, a number of nations, including the United States, had formed NATO, the North Atlantic Treaty Organization. The main idea behind NATO is for its members to share in the defense of Western Europe, an idea which Eisenhower strongly supported. The military part of NATO is called SHAPE,

Supreme Headquarters Allied Powers Europe. When SHAPE came into existence at the beginning of 1951, Eisenhower became its first commander.

For many years, people had been suggesting to Eisenhower that he try to become President of the United States. For a long time, his reaction was that he had no interest in the position. But enthusiasm for his candidacy was spreading, and his opposition to running was beginning to soften.

While he was in Europe with SHAPE, the momentum grew tremendously. Many were concluding individually: "I Like Ike." Finally, in February of 1952, he agreed to run. When he returned to the United States early in June, he was a candidate for the presidency, seeking the nomination of the Republican Party, whose convention was less than two months away.

Winning the nomination would be the hard part. When Eisenhower arrived in Chicago for the convention—the first one covered live on national television—his nomination was still uncertain because Senator Robert Taft of Ohio, the other major candidate, had much support among an influential part of the Republican Party known as the Old Guard. Even so, with help from Senator Henry Cabot Lodge of Massachusetts, and others, Eisenhower was nominated. He went to call on Senator Taft right away. Through the years, he had learned the great value of teamwork, and he wanted to waste no time in trying to make Taft and his supporters allies.

The next task was to select a running mate, a candidate for the vice presidency. With the goal of having a ticket balanced in politically important ways, Eisenhower selected, and the convention nominated, Senator Richard M. Nixon of California. He provided balance because, in comparison to Eisenhower, he was closer to the Old Guard, from the Far West, and younger.

In 1952, Eisenhower ran America's last whistle-stop presidential campaign, travelling by train to cities and towns throughout the nation. At stop after stop, Ike and Mamie would appear on the rear platform of the caboose and greet the crowd. Ike would give a speech and, of course, his famous grin. The whistle would sound, and off they would go to the next place. Eisenhower visited forty-five states during the campaign.

On election day, Ike defeated his Democratic rival, Adlai E. Stevenson of Illinois, by a substantial margin, and became President-elect.

Victory at the Republican
Convention for Richard
M. Nixon and Ike. Their
wives, Pat and Mamie,
share the excitement.

"I Like Ike" was the
popular campaign
slogan.

Ike travelled around
America on his whistle-
stop tour.

Thirty-fourth President

After the election, Eisenhower had two and one-half months in which to prepare for the presidency. He knew that whatever success he was going to have as President depended largely upon the people invited to join his administration. Therefore, he gave prompt attention to selecting them, especially the members of the Cabinet. Most members of the Cabinet are heads of the federal government's main departments such as the Department of Defense, the Department of the Treasury, and the Department of Justice.

When the building of the team was well in hand, Eisenhower travelled halfway around the world to Korea to fulfill a promise made during the campaign. United States forces were at war in Korea. The war had started in June of 1950 when North Korea, which was under Communist rule, had invaded South Korea. U.S. troops were there, as part of a United Nations mission, to help South Korea defend itself.

Knowing that, as President, he would have to deal with the Korean War, Eisenhower wanted to see it for himself. While in Korea, despite snow and extremely cold weather, he spent time with troops in the front lines and, in general, made a careful inspection. He drew his own conclusions about the fighting and about the best course for ending it.

January 20, 1953 was the day of Eisenhower's inauguration. Not long after taking office, Eisenhower realized that despite all the attention, being President also had its lonely, isolated side. To balance the demands of the presidency, Eisenhower had his family, his friends, and his recreational interests. One convenient getaway was the presidential retreat in Maryland. President Roosevelt had named it Shangri-La. President Eisenhower renamed it Camp David in honor of his first grandchild.

Eisenhower himself had a group of close friends with whom he enjoyed spending time. He referred to them as "the gang." Often they would join him to play golf or bridge when he wanted a break from the very substantial daily pressures of the presidency. He appreciated their friendship.

On January 20, 1953, Dwight D. Eisenhower was sworn in as the Thirty-fourth President by Chief Justice of the Supreme Court Fred Vinson.

Ike promised to go to Korea if elected, and he did.

Later he wrote: "Any person enjoys his or her friends; a President needs them, perhaps more intensely at times than anything else."

Much of Eisenhower's attention as President was focused on America's foreign policy—its relationships with other nations. The main concern was the worldwide conflict between forces in favor of, and those—like America—opposed to, the expansion of Communism. This conflict was carried on mostly through the Cold War, but sometimes, as in the Korean War, there was actual fighting.

A popular idea about the conflict with Communism was called the "domino" theory. It held that countries would fall to Communism similarly to the way in which dominoes standing in a row fall, one after another, once the first one has been pushed. The approach towards Communism, therefore, was to prevent its expansion.

About six months after he became President, a truce was arranged in Korea. Less than a year later, America faced new problems in Asia. Eisenhower's response was to support the creation of SEATO, the Southeast Asia Treaty Organization. SEATO's members, like NATO's, were dedicated to joint defense.

Eisenhower viewed the expansion of Communism as such a threat that he at times permitted the use of covert—undercover—action to fight it. In this way leaders were overthrown in Iran in 1953 and in Guatemala in 1954, two settings in which Communism was rapidly making gains.

Throughout his presidency he knew when it was wise not to have American troops begin some action because it could not be well finished. A major uprising against the Communist government did begin in Hungary during the fall of 1956, but, with the Soviet Union playing a major role, it was brutally put down. Although Eisenhower was very unhappy over the situation, his best judgment was that America was in no position to use military force to change it.

Also in the fall of 1956, Eisenhower surprised a large part of the world when he opposed three of America's best friends—Great Britain, France, and Israel—for their invasion of Egypt after it had taken over the Suez Canal. America took its case to the United Nations General Assembly, where its cease-fire resolution was passed by a vote of 64 to 5. Britain, France, Israel, Australia, and New Zealand were the only countries voting against it.

At Camp David with Ike and Mamie: John, Barbara, and their children, (left to right) Susan Elaine, Barbara Anne, and David. Mary Jean, their youngest child, was born later.

During a break from more serious discussions, Khrushchev and Eisenhower share a laugh outside at Camp David.

Camp David in the mountains of Maryland

Queen Elizabeth II and President Eisenhower at the opening of the St. Lawrence Seaway

◄ A ship goes through the Dwight D. Eisenhower Lock near Massena, N.Y. The locks act like elevators, raising and lowering water levels so that ships can pass through.

Construction of a vast network of interstate highways was begun during the Eisenhower presidency.

Representatives from the smaller, less wealthy nations of the world were delighted that America had sided with one of them in this crucial situation and said so. Eisenhower had simply done what he thought was morally right.

Eisenhower was also concerned with many issues at home. One of the largest during his first two years in office involved Senator Joseph McCarthy of Wisconsin. Through methods deeply in conflict with basic American notions of fairness, McCarthy whipped many people into hysterics about the dangers America faced from some of its own citizens in its struggle against Communism. Many outraged Americans wanted Eisenhower to criticize McCarthy strongly, but Eisenhower did not want to give him all the attention a big public argument with the President would provide. So, for the most part, he worked quietly, behind the scenes, to bring the damage McCarthy was creating under control. Eventually the Senate sharply criticized McCarthy—it censured him—and the days of his power were over.

In November of 1956, Eisenhower stood for election to a second term. Ordinarily the decision to run would have been more or less automatic for such a popular President, but because he had suffered a heart attack in September of 1955, the matter took some careful thought. In February, he decided to run. This time the Republican Party nominated him by acclamation. Adlai Stevenson was once more the Democratic Party's nominee. In November, Eisenhower was elected to a second term.

One of the many programs for which Eisenhower is well known is the Interstate Highway System. Begun in 1956, the system has since grown to have over 42,000 miles of highways crisscrossing the nation. In 1973, Congress named one section of it, extending between Washington, D.C. and San Francisco, the Dwight D. Eisenhower Highway. It closely follows the route of the convoy with which Eisenhower travelled in 1919.

The St. Lawrence Seaway is another major transportation project with which Eisenhower was closely associated. In 1954 he signed the law making America a coparticipant with Canada. In June of 1959, President Eisenhower and Queen Elizabeth II dedicated the Seaway. It enables a ship starting at Duluth, Minnesota to travel all the way to the Atlantic Ocean, by passing through sixteen locks.

As President, Eisenhower dealt with important issues in civil rights. He completed the desegregation of the armed forces, begun by Truman, arranged the desegregation of public facilities in Washington, D.C., and made efforts to improve voting rights for those people denied them. When Arkansas' Governor Orval Faubus would not take action to control a mob interfering with integration at Little Rock's Central High School, Eisenhower sent federal troops to do it. Despite his firmness in this instance, he has still received a good deal of criticism for not using the strength of his position to promote integration in the nation's public schools actively and broadly.

Competition with the Soviet Union was a constant theme during Eisenhower's presidency. In October of 1957, the Russians were the first to reach space; their satellite was named Sputnik. America's response led to the creation of NASA in 1958, and, eventually, to the nation's space program.

During his presidency, Eisenhower had three summit meetings with Nikita Khrushchev. Stalin had died in 1953, and Khrushchev was the next Soviet leader. The summits took place in Geneva in 1955, in the United States in 1959, and in Paris in 1960. The summit in Geneva served to reduce tensions, but the one in Paris certainly did not. Shortly before it, an American plane called a U-2, flying on an intelligence-gathering mission, had gone down far within the Soviet Union. Not suspecting that the Soviet Union had captured the pilot alive and had recovered the remains of the plane, Eisenhower issued an incorrect explanation and became stuck with and stung by it. Khrushchev disrupted the summit almost before it got started. The U-2 incident was especially unfortunate for Eisenhower because it took away his last major chance to improve relations with the Soviet Union.

As his presidency was drawing to a close, Eisenhower delivered his Farewell Address. It is remembered best for its straightforward warning of the danger the nation would risk if it allowed the military-industrial complex —those in government who buy, and those major corporations which sell, expensive military equipment like airplanes and aircraft carriers—to become too powerful. It was a thoughtful and deeply patriotic message from an American who profoundly loved his country.

In the election of 1960, John F. Kennedy narrowly defeated Richard M. Nixon, and on January 20, 1961, Eisenhower's presidency ended, and Kennedy's began. As President, Eisenhower had kept the nation out of war. He had been a faithful and trustworthy leader. After half a century of hard work, it was time for his retirement. He more than deserved it.

Ike greets President-elect John F. Kennedy on the White House steps. They were the oldest and the youngest Presidents ever elected up to 1960.

The White House, home to the Eisenhowers from January 1953 to January 1961.

Final Years

When Eisenhower's presidency ended, he and Mamie went to live at their farm in Gettysburg, Pennsylvania. They had bought it in 1950, and it was the only home they ever owned. It is located next to the famous battlefield of the Civil War and not far from the land on which Eisenhower's grandfather, Jacob, had lived before heading west.

Eisenhower remained so busy that, commenting upon the notion of retirement, he said, "My wife thinks it's just a word in the dictionary." Presidents Kennedy, Johnson, and Nixon all sought his help. He travelled to Europe to film a documentary to commemorate the twentieth anniversary of D-Day. He had an office at Gettysburg College, and he received a huge volume of mail.

He wrote. With help from others, notably his son John, he prepared his memoirs from the presidency, a work of two volumes called *The White House Years*.

After suffering a second heart attack in 1965, Eisenhower began to sense that his remaining time was short. He arranged to have Icky's body moved from Denver to the Place of Meditation at the Eisenhower Center in Abilene, where he and Mamie would also be buried.

Although he had to spend most of the last year of his life in a hospital, he was still interested and involved in the affairs of the world. Speaking via television from the hospital, he addressed the 1968 convention of the Republican Party in Miami. On his seventy-eighth birthday, the Army Band gathered outside to play for him.

Right before the Army-Navy football game in 1968, he sent West Point's coach a telegram for the team: "For 364 days out of the year it is Army, Navy, Air Force, forever. Today it is Army, Army, Army. My heart, though somewhat damaged, will be riding with you and the team. Good luck!!"

Not long before entering the hospital, he had still been playing golf. One day he got "the thrill of a lifetime." He had made a hole in one.

Ike and Mamie enjoy being back on the farm. ◄

Ike dons a parade dress hat while a West Point cadet looks on. ►

Golfing and fishing were among Ike's favorite pastimes. ►

The farm in Gettysburg, Pennsylvania served as the Eisenhowers' retirement home. ▲

On March 28, 1969, with Mamie, John, and his grandson David at his bedside, Dwight David Eisenhower died. Near the end, he had summed up most simply: "I've always loved my wife. I've always loved my children. I've always loved my grandchildren. I've always loved my country."

After the funeral in Washington, D.C., he went home to the heartland of America from where he had come, home to Abilene. There, near the small farm of his childhood, he was buried. Today, people from all over America and throughout the world visit the Eisenhower Center in Abilene. They come to see the Eisenhower Home, the Library, Museum, Visitors' Center, and Place of Meditation. They come to honor the memory of this great man.